Easy Meals
COOKBOOK

Kitchen Fare
Wauwatosa, Wisconsin

Contents

ISBN 0-8249-3710-4

COPYRIGHT © MCMLXXXI BY KITCHEN FARE
WAUWATOSA, WI 53226
ALL RIGHTS RESERVED. PRINTED AND BOUND IN U.S.A.

Pictured opposite:
Cheese Dill Weed Spread, p. 4

Appetizers and Soups

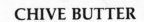

CHEESE DILL WEED SPREAD

2 T. butter
1 T. flour
2 T. sugar
1 c. milk
2 egg yolks
1 t. dry mustard
¾ lb. grated cheddar cheese
1 t. dill weed

Melt butter; add flour, sugar and milk. Cook until slightly thickened. Add yolks, then mustard, cheese and dill weed. Refrigerate in a sealed jar. Serve with crackers and raw vegetables.

HOT CREAM CHEESE DIP

1 8-oz. pkg. cream cheese
2 t. milk
1 3-oz. pkg. dried beef, shredded
1 t. onion salt
½ t. mustard
2 t. chopped green pepper
½ c. sour cream
¼ c. chopped parsley
¼ c. coarsely chopped nuts

Mix together all ingredients except nuts. Place in small casserole, sprinkling nuts on top. Bake at 350° for 15 minutes. Serve with crackers or toast. Serve hot.

CHIVE BUTTER

1 c. butter
5 T. chopped chives
2 T. prepared mustard

Combine all ingredients; mix until well blended. Use as a dip for raw vegetables such as celery, carrot strips, cucumber, green pepper, or onions.

GUACAMOLE DIP

1 ripe avocado, mashed
2 hard-boiled eggs, finely chopped
Salt
Pepper
Garlic salt
¼ c. mayonnaise
¼ c. sour cream
Dash of cayenne

Combine all ingredients, whipping until smooth. Serve with corn chips.

PARTY DIP

½ c. sherry wine or brandy
1 pkg. onion soup
1 c. sour cream

Mix soup and wine together and let stand for one hour. Gently fold in sour cream. Top with a sprinkle of paprika. Use as a vegetable dip.

EASY SHRIMP SPREAD

1 8-oz. pkg. cream cheese
¼ c. cream
½ t. chopped onion
2 t. lemon juice
1½ t. Worcestershire sauce
2 4½-oz. cans tiny broken shrimp

Combine all ingredients in a blender or mixer; whip until smooth and well blended. Serve on crackers.

MOCK CHOPPED LIVER

1 1-lb. can cut green beans
½ c. walnuts
Vegetable oil
1 onion, chopped
2 hard-boiled eggs, chopped
1 t. mayonnaise

Finely chop green beans and nuts. Sauté chopped onion in a small amount of oil until soft. Blend all ingredients together. Serve with baked toast or crackers.

SHRIMP BUTTER

Add shredded shrimp or tiny ones to creamed butter. Season with salt, lemon juice, and a little onion salt. Spread on small circles of bread, dusting the edges with minced parsley or chives.

DUCHESS PUFFS

⅓ c. shortening
1 t. salt
1 c. boiling water
1 c. flour
3 eggs, beaten

Mix as in order given; add eggs one at a time, beating well after each. Drop by teaspoons onto buttered cookie sheet. Bake 400° for 8 minutes. Turn heat to 350° and bake for 12 minutes more. Puffs should be puffy and light brown in color. Fill with chicken salad, seafood or egg salad. Can be made larger and used for desserts, eclairs or cream puffs. Makes 30 small puffs or 18 larger dessert puffs. Can be frozen without filling. Defrost in refrigerator and then fill.

SPICED RIPE OLIVES

1 6-oz. can large ripe olives with juice
1 small clove garlic
1 bay leaf
Few dill seeds
2 T. olive oil
1 T. pickling spice

Combine all ingredients in large jar. Cover and place in refrigerator for several days. Drain and serve.

EASY ONION CANAPÉ

Spread rounds of rye bread or wafer with cream cheese. Place a thin slice of Bermuda onion on the cream cheese, then top with a little mayonnaise. Sprinkle with Parmesan cheese and a little paprika. Broil 3 minutes.

BRANDIED ALMONDS

2 c. blanched almonds
¼ c. butter or margarine
2¼ c. confectioners' sugar
2 T. sherry wine
2 T. brandy

Place almonds on a cookie sheet and toast in a 350° oven until browned. Cream together butter, sugar, sherry and brandy. While nuts are still hot, mix them with the sugar mixture. When well coated, spread out to cool. Pecans can also be used.

EASY SHRIMP AND CHEESE

Split peeled and deveined fresh, raw shrimp lengthwise. Spread one half of each shrimp with Roquefort cheese softened with a little cream. Press shrimp halves together and dip in slightly beaten egg, then in dry bread crumbs. Fry in hot oil until golden brown. Can be fried in advance and kept hot in a warm oven until serving time.

CHAMPAGNE DELIGHT

1 ⅘-qt. bottle pink champagne
1 qt. lemon sherbet

Stir sherbet into sparkling pink champagne and freeze in freezing trays. Serve in sherbet glasses with half a straw. Garnish with whole strawberry with the cap left on. Partially cut through the berry from the pointed end. Hook berry over the edge of the glass with the cap pointed up. Serves 6 to 8 guests.

SPRING COCKTAIL

Frost wine glasses by dipping the rims into lemon juice and then into red, green or yellow sugar. Fill glasses with May wine and float a large strawberry with the cap left on.

COLD WINE SOUP

5 c. rich beef consommé
1 c. dry white wine

Combine consommé and wine. Chill and serve with a slice of lemon. Serves 8 to 10 guests.

CREAM OF BROCCOLI SOUP

2 10-oz. pkgs. chopped broccoli
1 onion, sliced
1 small bunch celery, diced
1 T. butter
½ c. water
2 T. rice
½ c. cream
½ c. milk

Cook broccoli according to package directions. Drain, reserving broth. Place onion, celery, butter, water and broccoli broth with rice in a kettle and simmer 25 minutes, or until rice is tender. Place in a blender, adding cream and milk; blend until smooth. Pour into a pan and slowly heat, but do not boil. Serve with croutons. Serves 6 to 8 guests.

*Pictured opposite:
Pumpkin Bread, p. 10*

CHEESE SOUP

1 T. melted butter
1 T. flour
1 c. chicken broth
2 c. milk
2 T. chopped onion
1 t. butter
¾ c. grated cheddar cheese

Add flour to the melted butter, blending well. Slowly add broth, stirring until smooth. Stir in milk. Sauté chopped onion in 1 teaspoon butter; add to sauce. Warm sauce, being careful not to boil. Add cheese, stirring to melt. Serve with paprika.

AVOCADO SOUP

1 ripe avocado
2 c. chicken stock or 2 chicken bouillon
    cubes dissolved in 2 c. water
⅓ c. milk
    Sherry
    Paprika

Mash avocado; add to chicken stock and milk. Heat but do not boil. Add a dash of sherry and sprinkle with paprika. Serve with a crisp tortilla or croutons. May be heated or served cold.

CHILLED CARROT SOUP

¼ c. shortening
1 large onion, cubed
6 carrots, diced
3 c. chicken broth
¾ t. curry
1½ t. salt
1 c. light cream

Melt shortening. Add onion and carrots; sauté, but do not brown. Add chicken broth and curry. Place in blender, blending until smooth. Add cream; chill. Top with parsley and serve with wafers or toast.

QUICK POTATO SOUP

2 c. dry potato buds
4 c. hot water
1 t. salt
1 large onion, finely chopped
4 slices bacon, fried and chopped

Make mashed potatoes according to directions on package but eliminate the milk. Add hot water and salt to potatoes. Sauté onion in bacon grease and add to potato mixture. Top with minced parsley. Serves 4 to 6.

CHERRY SOUP

1 1-qt. can red or black pitted cherries
1 c. claret or sherry wine or orange juice
1½ t. cinnamon
¼ c. sugar
½ lemon, finely sliced
2 c. water
1 T. cornstarch mixed with ¼ c. water

Drain cherries, reserving juice. In a saucepan, combine cherry juice, orange juice or wine, cinnamon, sugar, water and lemon slices. Simmer for 15 minutes. Strain and add cornstarch which has been blended with the ¼ c. water. Cook, stirring occasionally, for 10 minutes. Serve with a dab of sour cream if desired.

SHERRIED BOUILLON ON THE ROCKS

12 ice cubes
2 10½-oz. cans condensed bouillon
6 T. sherry wine
    Rind of 1 lemon

Place 2 ice cubes in each of six glasses. Divide undiluted bouillon between the glasses. Add 1 tablespoon wine to each glass. Garnish with a small twist of lemon rind. Serve at once.

Breads

QUICK BRAIDS

1 pkg. refrigerated crescent roll dough
1 8-oz. jar raspberry or peach preserves
½ c. flour
¼ c. sugar
2 T. butter or margarine
1 egg yolk
1 t. water

Divide contents of dough package in half. Roll each half into an oblong. Place on buttered foil on cookie sheet. With a sharp knife, cut slits from the outer edge to 1½ inches from the center. Spread jam down the center of each piece. Mix together flour, sugar and butter. Sprinkle half over the jam. Crisscross cut side sections over jam to simulate braids. Repeat for the second braid. Brush tops with egg yolk mixed with water and sprinkle with remainder of topping. Bake at 350° for 15 minutes. Top with a thin Sugar Icing. When slicing, cut at an angle. Makes 2 braids.

SUGAR ICING

½ c. confectioners' sugar
¼ t. almond extract
1 t. warm water

Mix all ingredients together. Add more water if needed to thin icing or more sugar if icing is too thin.

BREAKFAST PUFFS

1 7¼-oz. pkg. yellow cake mix
¾ c. water
½ t. nutmeg
¼ c. vegetable oil
1 egg
3 T. melted margarine
¼ c. sugar
1 T. cinnamon

Mix together cake mix, water, nutmeg, oil and egg, blending well. Fill paper-lined muffin tins two-thirds full. Bake at 350° for 20 minutes. Combine melted margarine, sugar and cinnamon. When puffs are done, dip into melted margarine mixture.

ZUCCHINI BREAD

3 c. flour
2 t. cinnamon
2 t. baking soda
1 t. salt
1 c. chopped nuts
3 eggs
2 c. sugar
1 c. vegetable oil
2 t. vanilla
2 c. grated zucchini

Stir dry ingredients together. Add remaining ingredients, beating well after each addition. Pour batter into two well-greased bread pans. Bake at 350° for 1 hour.

FRENCH BREADS IN MINIATURE

1 pkg. country style biscuits
1 egg yolk plus 1 t. water

Divide package of biscuits into three parts. Stand on side on buttered cookie sheet. Pinch ends and form into the shape of a small loaf of French bread. Brush tops with slightly beaten egg yolk mixed with water.

CHOCOLATE ALMOND TEA BREAD

½ c. chopped toasted almonds
¼ c. butter
⅔ c. sugar
2 eggs
1¼ c. flour
2½ t. baking powder
1 t. salt
½ t. cinnamon
¼ t. nutmeg
¼ t. almond flavoring
2½ c. whole wheat flour
½ c. milk
1 1-oz. square bitter chocolate, grated

Blend together all ingredients until smooth. Place in a well-buttered bread pan. Bake at 325° for 50 to 55 minutes. Let stand about 10 minutes before unmolding. Cool before cutting.

PUMPKIN BREAD

⅓ c. shortening
1⅓ c. sugar
2 eggs
1 c. canned pumpkin
1⅔ c. flour
1 t. baking soda
¼ t. baking powder
¾ t. salt
½ t. cinnamon
½ t. nutmeg
⅓ c. water
½ t. vanilla
½ c. chopped nuts

Mix all ingredients together, beating well. Place batter in a buttered bread pan. Bake at 350° for 1½ hours. Cool and slice.

CALIFORNIA MUFFINS

1 c. boiling water
2½ t. baking soda
½ c. shortening
1 c. sugar
1 egg
1 egg yolk
2 c. buttermilk
2½ c. flour
½ t. salt
2 c. all-bran cereal
½ c. chopped nuts
1 c. chopped dates or raisins

Dissolve soda in boiling water; cool. Cream together shortening and sugar. Add water and 1 egg, beating well. Stir in remaining ingredients in order given, beating well after each addition. Store in refrigerator overnight or up to six weeks. Bake at 375° for 20 minutes. Makes 3 dozen muffins.

*Pictured opposite:
California Muffins*

ELEPHANT TEARS

1 can crescent roll dough
1 stick margarine
1¼ c. sugar
3 T. cinnamon
1 egg yolk beaten with 1 t. water

Butter two foil-lined cookie sheets. Mix sugar and cinnamon. Melt margarine. Separate roll dough into 2 oblongs, pressing perforations to seal. Spread with margarine and sprinkle with a little sugar and cinnamon. Starting at the long side, roll up as for a jelly roll. Cut each into 12 slices. Dip each into melted margarine, sugar and cinnamon. Place cut side down on tin, pressing with the palm until very thin. Brush with egg yolk mix and top with remaining sugar and cinnamon. Bake at 350° for 10 minutes. Makes 24 Tears.

FILLED COFFEE CAKE

1 pkg. crescent roll dough
¼ c. melted butter
¼ c. sugar
1½ T. cinnamon
½ c. flour

Divide roll dough into two parts. Press each half into a buttered 6" x 8" pan. Combine remaining ingredients, mixing until crumbly. Sprinkle this on top of each cake which has first been brushed with melted butter. Bake at 350° for 15 to 20 minutes. When cake has cooled, slice each cake lengthwise and carefully lift off the top. Spread the bottom layers with Filling. Replace top and sprinkle with confectioners' sugar. Refrigerate until serving time.

FILLING

2½ T. flour
½ c. milk
½ c. margarine
1 c. confectioners' sugar
1 t. vanilla

Cook flour and milk to a thick paste. Cool. Cream margarine, sugar and vanilla. Gradually add cooled paste, beating well in mixer.

SQUASH MUFFINS

1 c. mashed, cooked squash, drained
¾ c. brown sugar
½ c. softened butter
1 egg, beaten
1¾ c. flour
1 t. baking powder
¼ t. salt
¼ c. chopped pecans

Mix all ingredients together, beating well. Fill buttered muffin tins a little over half full. Bake at 375° for 20 minutes. Makes 16 to 18 muffins.

COFFEE KUCHEN

2 c. flour
2 c. brown sugar
½ c. butter
⅓ c. flour
1 egg
1 c. buttermilk
1 t. baking soda
1 t. cinnamon

Blend flour, brown sugar, and butter until crumbly. Set aside ¾ cup of the mixture to use later. Add remaining ingredients and mix only until moistened. Pour batter into a 9" x 13" buttered pan. Sprinkle reserved mixture on top. Bake at 325° for 50 to 60 minutes.

OATMEAL DATE BREAD

1 c. quick-cooking oatmeal
1 c. hot water
½ c. shortening
½ c. brown sugar
½ c. sugar
2 eggs
½ t. cinnamon
1 t. baking soda
½ t. cloves
½ t. salt
½ c. chopped nuts
½ c. chopped dates

Pour hot water over oatmeal; cool. Add oatmeal to rest of ingredients and beat well. Place in a well-buttered bread tin. Bake at 350° for 1 hour. Can be baked in two smaller bread tins. Flavor improves if tightly wrapped for a day.

APPLE STRUDEL

½ c. butter
2 c. flour
1 t. salt
1 t. sugar
½ t. baking powder
½ c. sour cream
¼ c. melted butter
4 apples, finely chopped
1½ t. cinnamon
½ c. sugar
1 egg yolk mixed with 1 t. water

Cut butter into flour, salt, sugar and baking powder. Stir in sour cream, mixing thoroughly. Divide dough into four equal portions. Roll each portion into an 8" x 10" rectangle. Spread with melted butter. Combine cinnamon and sugar. Divide chopped apple among rectangles, then sprinkle with sugar and cinnamon mixture. Roll up as for a jelly roll. Place on a buttered cookie sheet. Brush tops of strudels with the egg yolk-water mixture. Sprinkle additional cinnamon-sugar on top. Bake at 400° for 10 minutes. Reduce heat to 350° and bake 25 minutes longer. Makes 4 strudels.

THIN ICING

1½ c. confectioners' sugar
1 t. almond extract
1½ T. milk or water

Combine all ingredients, stirring until smooth. Drizzle over top of strudel.

DUTCH APPLE KUCHEN

¾ c. flour
1 T. sugar
¼ t. baking powder
6 T. butter
¼ t. salt
½ c. chopped almonds
3 egg yolks
1 c. sugar
1 c. sour cream
6 apples, peeled, cored and chopped

Mix together the flour, sugar, baking powder, butter and salt. Pat mixture into a buttered 7" x 11" pie plate. Set aside. Mix together almonds, egg yolks, sugar and sour cream, blending well. Stir in apples. Pour apple mixture onto the unbaked crust. Bake at 250° for 30 minutes.

PEACH OR RASPBERRY STRUDEL

2¼ c. flour
1 c. sour cream
¼ c. sugar
1 c. butter or margarine
½ t. salt
½ c. chopped nuts
2 c. raspberry or peach preserves

Combine all ingredients except preserves; mix together. Chill dough for 1 hour. Divide into four equal portions and roll out each into an oblong shape. Spread with preserves; then roll up as a jelly roll. Place on buttered cookie sheet. Make a slit on top, one inch from each end. Bake at 375° for 20 minutes. Top with Thin Icing. Makes 4 strudels.

WHIPPED BUTTER

1 lb. sweet or salted butter
1 egg
¼ c. heavy cream

Have butter at room temperature. Combine butter and egg. Beat at high speed about 5 minutes. Add cream and beat another 10 minutes until very light and fluffy. Fill two 1-pound jars and store in refrigerator.

Pancakes, Omelets and Quiches

GERMAN PANCAKE

3 eggs
½ t. salt
½ c. flour
½ c. milk

Beat eggs; add rest of ingredients and mix only until smooth. Pour into a well-buttered iron skillet, and refrigerate overnight. Bake pancake in a 450° oven for 30 minutes. Pancake should be puffed up and light brown. If it isn't, bake an additional 5 to 10 minutes.

PANCAKES SKYSCRAPER EN FLAMBÉ

1½ c. brown sugar
¼ c. honey
1 T. lemon juice
2 t. water
½ c. rum

Combine all ingredients, mixing until smooth. Spread a little on each pancake or crepe and stack six together. Pour warmed rum over stack. Bring to the table and light. When serving, slice into wedges.

RICE PANCAKES

1 c. cooked rice
1 c. milk
1 T. vegetable oil
1 c. flour
1½ t. sugar
2 t. baking powder

Combine all ingredients, blending well. Fry as for pancakes.

FEATHER PANCAKES

1 egg
¾ c. milk
2 T. vegetable oil
1 c. flour
½ t. salt
2 T. sugar
2 T. baking powder

Mix together all ingredients, blending well. Fry as for pancakes.

Pictured opposite: German Pancake

BAKED SCRAMBLED EGGS

6 eggs, beaten
⅓ c. milk
1 t. salt
1 t. pepper
¼ lb. American cheese, cubed

Mix ingredients in order given. Bake in a well-buttered casserole in a 350° oven for 30 minutes, or until puffy and when a knife is inserted, it comes out clean.

MATZO-MEAL PANCAKES

½ c. matzo meal
¾ c. cold water
3 eggs, separated
½ t. salt

Soak meal in cold water for 15 minutes. Beat egg yolks with salt until very light and fluffy. Beat egg whites until stiff. Fold the mixtures together. Fry as pancakes in oil or butter. Makes 8 fluffy cakes. Should be eaten immediately as they deflate.

STRAWBERRY RUM OMELET

8 eggs
2 T. milk
1½ T. sugar
½ t. salt
1 T. butter
½ c. strawberries
¼ c. rum

Beat eggs; add milk, sugar and salt. Melt butter in a 10" skillet. Add egg mixture and cook over low heat. Lift edges with a fork, allowing liquid to seep to bottom of pan. When all is set, add strawberries and fold omelet in half. Place on warmed tray or platter. Pour slightly warmed rum over and light. Serve when flames die.

CREAMY EGGS

6 eggs
½ c. sour cream
1 t. prepared mustard
1 t. salt
1 t. pepper
2 T. minced onion
2 T. minced parsley
2 T. melted butter

Blend together all ingredients except butter. Pour butter in a frying pan, then add egg mixture. Stir gently over moderate heat as for scrambled eggs.

MUSHROOM OMELET

6 eggs
½ egg shell water for each egg
Salt and pepper to taste
1 4½-oz. can sliced mushrooms
1 T. minced parsley

Beat eggs with water and salt and pepper; add parsley and mushrooms. Place in a 10-inch skillet with two tablespoons melted butter. Bake in a 350° oven 8 to 10 minutes. Lift up edges, fold and roll over and serve. Serves 5 to 6 guests. Minced shrimp can be added in place of the mushrooms.

FLUFFY OMELET

2 T. butter
6 eggs, separated
3 T. flour
¼ t. salt
¼ t. cream of tartar

Heat butter in electric skillet at 300° for 10 minutes. Beat egg yolks with flour, 3 tablespoons water and salt. Beat the egg whites with cream of tartar until stiff. Fold the two mixtures together and pour into warmed skillet. Cover and bake for 10 minutes. May be served with fruit and sour cream. Serves 4 to 6.

EGG FOO YUNG

4 eggs
¾ lb. chopped, cooked chicken or turkey
½ can bean sprouts, drained
1 green onion, chopped
½ stalk of celery, chopped
  Salt
  Pepper
  Vegetable oil

Slightly beat eggs. Stir in cooked chicken or turkey, bean sprouts, green onion, celery, salt and pepper to taste. Cover bottom of a 6" skillet with oil and heat. Pour ¼ of mixture into pan and cook over low heat until set. Turn carefully and cook other side. Serve with brown sauce. Serves 4.

BROWN SAUCE

1 T. cornstarch
¼ t. sugar
1 t. soy sauce
1½ c. cold chicken broth
  Salt and pepper
1 small can sliced mushrooms or sliced water chestnuts

Combine all ingredients. Cook and stir over medium heat until mixture comes to a boil and starts to thicken. Add drained mushrooms or water chestnuts.

CHINESE FRIED RICE

1 egg
2 T. butter
1 c. cooked rice
⅓ c. diced onion
2 to 3 T. soy sauce
¼ c. water

Sauté onion and rice until light brown. Add slightly beaten egg, scrambling until fully cooked. Combine soy sauce and water and add to rice mixture.

MATZO-MEAL DUMPLINGS

2 eggs, separated
1 T. chicken fat
¼ t. salt
½ t. baking powder
¼ t. nutmeg
½ c. matzo meal

Beat egg yolks until light. Add melted chicken fat, salt, baking powder, nutmeg and meal. Beat egg whites until stiff and fold in last. Form into balls about ½ to 1 inch in diameter. Refrigerate for one hour to allow them to swell. Drop into rapidly boiling water and cook 15 minutes. Experiment with one ball first, dropping it in the boiling water. If it should fall apart, add a little more meal. If too much is added, dumplings will be heavy. Remove and serve with soup. Makes 36 balls.

CREPES FLORENTINE

1 pkg. frozen spinach, cooked and drained
4 T. margarine
6 T. flour
3 c. milk
1 t. salt
1 onion, chopped
1 c. shredded cheddar cheese
1 4½-oz. can shrimp

Prepare 18 large crepes. Melt margarine; add flour, blending well. Slowly stir in milk and simmer until thickened. Add salt, onion and cheese. Reserve 2 cups of the sauce. Add spinach to the remaining 1 cup sauce. Fill crepes with the spinach mixture; folding in the ends, roll crepes. Place in a buttered dish, open side down. Add shrimp to the reserved sauce and pour over the crepes. Garnish with large sautéed mushrooms.

CREPES

4 eggs
1 egg yolk
¾ c. milk
¼ c. water
1 c. flour
1 t. salt

Beat all ingredients together, blending well. Place in the refrigerator overnight. Put a small amount of oil in a small frypan. Pour enough batter in to cover the bottom when the pan is tilted. Fry quickly on one side only. Turn out onto paper toweling, placing browned side up. Can be filled with cheese, meat or fruits. Makes 18 large crepes or 30 medium ones.

QUICK QUICHE LORRAINE

1 8" baked pie shell
4 large slices Swiss cheese, cut into strips
2 eggs
1 c. light cream
½ t. salt
¼ t. nutmeg
Pinch red pepper

Place strips of cheese in pie shell. Beat eggs with a fork; add cream and seasonings, blending well. Pour into pie shell. Bake 5 minutes in a 450° oven. Reduce heat to 400° and bake 5 to 10 minutes more, or until firm.

QUICHE LORRAINE

2 c. thinly sliced onion
3 T. butter
1 c. sour cream
2 eggs, slightly beaten
1 t. salt
¼ t. pepper
Pinch of ginger
¼ t. nutmeg
2 T. caraway seed
½ lb. bacon, diced, fried and drained

Make Cream Cheese Pastry and line pie pan or 12 individual tins. Sauté onion in butter until golden; add remaining ingredients. Pour onto crust. Top with paprika. Bake at 450° for 10 minutes. Reduce heat to 350° and bake 30 minutes longer, or until knife inserted into custard comes out clean.

CREAM CHEESE PASTRY

¾ c. flour
½ t. salt
4 oz. cream cheese
½ c. butter

Stir salt into flour. Cut in cream cheese and butter. Roll out on lightly floured surface.

Pictured opposite:
Quiche Lorraine

BEEF CREPES WITH BLUE CHEESE

- 1 lb. ground beef
- ½ c. chopped onion
- 2 T. vegetable oil
- 1 egg
- ⅓ c. crumbled blue cheese
- ½ c. finely chopped ripe olives
- 1 c. sour cream
- 16 5-inch crepes or pancakes
  Salt
  Pepper

Brown beef and onion in oil. Mix slightly beaten egg with cheese and add to beef along with olives and sour cream. Simmer for 5 minutes, stirring constantly. Salt and pepper to taste. When mixture has cooled, fill crepes. Roll up and place on buttered cookie sheet. Brush tops with a little melted butter and bake in a 375° oven for 20 minutes. These can be frozen and popped into the oven for about 25 minutes. Can be served with a cheese or mushroom sauce.

Meat and Seafood

BAKED CHOP SUEY

- 2 lbs. ground beef
- 4 T. margarine or butter
- 3 onions, chopped
- 2 c. celery, cut diagonally
- 1 green pepper, diced
- 2 10½-oz. cans cream of chicken soup
- 1 10½-oz. can cream of mushroom soup
- 3 soup cans water
- 6 T. soy sauce
- 2 cans sliced water chestnuts
- 1 4-oz. can mushrooms
- 1 8-oz. can bean sprouts
- 1 c. rice
  Chow mein noodles

Brown meat in margarine; add onions, celery and green pepper. Sauté until onion is golden and celery is tender. Stir in remaining ingredients, except noodles, and blend well. Pour mixture in a well-buttered casserole; top with noodles. Bake in a 350° oven for 1½ hours. Serves 10 to 12.

HAMBURGER STROGANOFF

½ c. minced onion
¼ c. butter
2 lbs. ground beef
2 T. flour
2 t. salt
1 t. pepper
1 10½-oz. can undiluted mushroom soup
1 c. sour cream
1 10½-oz. can undiluted cream of
  chicken soup
  Chow mein noodles

Sauté minced onion in butter. Add beef and brown slightly. Add flour, seasonings, and soups. Simmer for 20 minutes. Add sour cream and serve over chow mein noodles. Serves 8 to 10 guests. Sliced water chestnuts can be added.

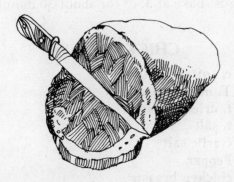

INDIVIDUAL MEAT LOAVES

1½ lbs. ground beef
1 egg
1 c. bread crumbs
1 onion, finely chopped
1¼ t. salt
¼ t. pepper
1½ c. tomato sauce
2 T. vinegar
2 T. prepared mustard
2 T. brown sugar
1 c. water

Combine beef, egg, bread crumbs, onion, salt and pepper, mixing well. Form into 6 tiny oblong loaves. Place on cookie sheet and brown under broiler for 7 to 8 minutes. Combine remaining ingredients, mixing well. Top meat loaves with sauce and broil 5 more minutes.

PORCUPINES

2 lbs. ground beef
1 egg
1 onion, finely chopped
½ c. rice
1 10½-oz. can tomato soup

Mix and shape in 1-inch balls. Brown in margarine on both sides. Place in a roaster and cover with undiluted soup. Bake at 350° for 1 hour.

MEAT LOAF UNUSUAL

1 lb. ground beef
1 small onion, chopped
1 egg
1 T. minced parsley
½ c. quick-cooking oatmeal
1 t. salt
¼ t. pepper

Mix well and place into a well-greased bread tin. Bake at 350° for 45 minutes.

SPAGHETTI AMORE

1 lb. spaghetti, cooked, drained,
  and rinsed
1 lb. ground beef
½ c. chopped onion
¼ c. chopped green pepper
2 T. butter
1 10½-oz. can undiluted cream of
  mushroom soup
1 10½-oz. can tomato soup
1 can water
1 clove garlic, minced
1 c. shredded cheddar cheese

Brown beef in butter with onion and green pepper. Stir in soups, water and garlic. Combine meat mixture with cooked spaghetti in a buttered 3-quart casserole. Top with shredded cheese. Bake at 350° for 30 minutes, or until bubbly.

CHICKEN ASPARAGUS ROLLS

PASTRY

1½ T. butter
1 c. flour
2 t. baking powder
¼ t. salt
½ t. sugar
⅓ c. milk

Sift together dry ingredients. Cut in butter. Add milk, mixing with a fork, until dough forms a ball. Set aside.

FILLING

¾ c. cooked chicken, finely cut up
½ t. salt
½ t. minced onion
2 T. butter
2 T. flour
1 c. milk
Salt
Pepper

Melt butter; add flour, milk, salt and pepper. Cook slowly until slightly thickened. Add chicken; cool. Roll pastry into a very thin rectangle; spread chicken filling over pastry. Roll up as for a jelly roll. Cut into 1" slices; place cut side down on buttered cookie sheet. Bake in a 450° oven for 20 minutes. Serve with the following sauce.

SAUCE

1 tall can asparagus with liquid
2 T. flour
½ c. milk
¼ c. diced pimiento

Drain asparagus liquid into saucepan. Dissolve flour in milk; add to asparagus liquid. Over low heat, stir until thickened. Add asparagus, cut into small pieces, and pimiento. Serve over chicken rolls.

BAKED CHICKEN

Place pieces of chicken on a large piece of foil. Top each piece with 1 teaspoon butter, 1 teaspoon dried onion soup mix, and 1 tablespoon cream. Wrap tightly in the foil. Bake in a 350° oven for 1 hour.

CHICKEN CLUB CASSEROLE

4 T. shortening
5 T. flour
1 c. chicken broth
1½ c. evaporated milk
1 t. salt
3 c. cooked rice
1½ c. diced, cooked chicken
1 4½-oz. can mushrooms
¼ c. chopped pimiento
¼ c. green pepper, diced
½ c. Sauterne
½ c. slivered almonds

Melt shortening; blend in flour. Stir in chicken broth. Slowly add milk and salt, stirring to combine smoothly. Simmer until sauce begins to thicken. Add remaining ingredients, except almonds. Place in a buttered casserole and top with slivered almonds. Bake at 350° for about 30 minutes.

CHICKEN KIEV

¼ c. softened butter
1 T. minced parsley
½ t. dried tarragon
½ t. salt
Garlic salt
Pepper
2 chicken breasts
Flour
1 beaten egg
Dry bread crumbs
Vegetable oil

Cream together the butter, parsley, tarragon, salt, garlic salt, and pepper. Divide into 4 portions; and shape each portion into a 2-inch finger. Freeze for 20 minutes. Bone, skin and cut in half the chicken breasts. Pound each to a ¼-inch thickness. Place the butter portion in the center of each chicken breast. Roll meat around butter, tucking in ends. Secure with a toothpick if necessary. Dust with flour, dip in beaten egg, and roll in bread crumbs. Cover and refrigerate 1 hour. Fry chicken in deep fat until golden brown, about 5 to 7 minutes. Be careful not to pierce the meat as the butter will run out.

Pictured opposite:
Ham Surprise, p.24

CHICKEN ALMOND LOAF

1 16-oz. loaf white bread
6 stalks celery, diced
2 onions, finely chopped
2 c. water
1 T. salt
  Pinch pepper
2 t. sage
2 eggs
¼ c. margarine
2 T. minced parsley
1 14½-oz. can evaporated milk
2 10½-oz. cans cream of mushroom soup
4 to 5 c. cooked, diced chicken
¼ c. slivered almonds

Cover bread with cold water then squeeze out the excess. Cook celery and onion in water until tender. Drain, and add to bread with seasonings, eggs, margarine and parsley. Line a well-buttered 6-cup casserole with the dressing, reserving 1½ cups for the top. Combine milk and soup, mixing well. Place chicken on top of dressing and cover with soup and milk. Put reserved dressing on top and dot with extra butter and a few slivered almonds. Bake 1 hour at 350°.

CHICKEN CURRY

½ c. vegetable oil
6 T. flour
2 c. water
2 c. thick applesauce
2½ t. curry powder
½ t. ginger
¼ c. lemon juice
4 c. diced, cooked chicken
5 c. cooked rice
  Shredded coconut

In a saucepan, heat oil; stir in flour. Slowly add water, stirring constantly. Add applesauce, spices and lemon juice. Layer chicken, rice, and sauce in buttered casserole. Finish with sauce on top. Sprinkle with shredded coconut. Bake at 350° for 45 minutes. Serve with small bowls filled with pineapple chunks, large raisins, salted nuts, dill weed, tomato wedges, fried onion rings and chutney. Serves 10 to 12.

CHICKEN IMPERIAL

1 c. bread crumbs
¼ c. Parmesan cheese
¼ c. chopped parsley
  Pinch of garlic salt
1 t. salt
  Pinch pepper
10 to 12 chicken legs with thighs
1½ c. melted butter or margarine

Combine crumbs, cheese, parsley, and seasonings. Dip each chicken leg into melted butter, then into crumb mixture. Place on buttered foil-lined pan. Bake at 350° for 1 hour.

PORK CHOPS IN BEER OR WINE

Brown chops with finely sliced onions. Add 1 cup beer or ½ cup wine and ½ cup tomato soup. Simmer 1 hour.

HAM SURPRISE

4 Idaho potatoes
2 egg yolks, beaten
½ t. salt
2 c. freshly sliced mushrooms
¼ c. minced onion
¼ c. diced green pepper
1 T. minced parsley
½ c. grated cheddar cheese
1½ lb. boiled ham, cut in chunks
¼ c. butter
½ c. flour
¼ c. water

Bake potatoes; when done, cut in halves. Scoop out centers, leaving the shell. Add egg yolks, and salt to potatoes. Beat until fluffy. Set aside. Melt butter and sauté mushrooms, onion, green pepper and parsley. Dissolve flour in water and add to mushroom mixture, stirring until slightly thickened. Put diced ham in the potato shell, top with thickened sauce and then whipped potato mixture. Sprinkle grated cheese on top of each potato. Bake 15 minutes at 375° or until slightly browned on top. Can be prepared in advance, and kept refrigerated until time to pop into the oven.

DEVILED EGG AND CRAB CASSEROLE

1½ c. sliced mushrooms
2 T. chopped onion
¼ c. butter or margarine
¼ c. flour
1 t. salt
½ t. paprika
2 c. milk
1 t. Worcestershire sauce
2 egg yolks, beaten
2 T. sherry wine
2 6½-oz. cans crab meat
3 hard-boiled eggs

Melt butter in saucepan; stir in flour, salt and paprika, blending well. Slowly stir in milk, stirring until smooth. Cool slightly. Stir a bit of the warm mixture into egg yolks. Add egg yolks, sherry, and Worcestershire sauce, along with mushrooms, chopped onion, and flaked crab meat. Place in a 1½-quart casserole. Cut hard-boiled eggs in halves; remove yolks. Mash yolks and mix with a little mayonnaise. Refill egg halves and place on top of the casserole. Heat for about 15-20 minutes in a 350° oven. A little crab meat can be used on top of deviled eggs. This can be made in advance and refrigerated until time to pop into the oven.

BAKED CLAMS

3 T. butter
2 T. chopped onion
1 T. chopped parsley
  Juice of ½ lemon
¼ c. dry white wine
  Salt
2 c. minced clams
½ c. melted butter
  Bread crumbs

Combine first six ingredients. Simmer until liquid is reduced by one-half. Add minced clams. Brown bread crumbs in butter. Divide clam mixture among buttered individual serving shells and top with crumbs. Brown under broiler.

BAKED SALMON

1 T. butter
1 T. flour
½ c. milk
1 egg
1 T. lemon juice
½ c. mayonnaise
1 c. raw grated carrot
1 green pepper, chopped
1 1-lb. can salmon, drained and flaked
2 slices white bread, buttered and cubed

Melt butter; add flour, stirring well. Slowly stir in milk; cook until slightly thickened. Add egg, lemon juice, mayonnaise, carrots, green pepper and salmon. Pour in a buttered 4-cup casserole and top with cubed bread. Bake in a 350° oven for 25 minutes.

AVOCADO STUFFED WITH CRAB MEAT

2 T. butter
2 T. flour
1 lb. cooked crab meat, flaked
1 c. milk
¼ t. Worcestershire sauce
2 T. chopped pimiento
2 large green olives, chopped
¼ c. grated cheese
3 avocados, halved

Melt butter; stir in flour until well blended. Add milk, a little at a time, stirring constantly. Cook over low heat until thickened. Add remaining ingredients except grated cheese and avocados. Fill avocado halves with mixture. Top with grated cheese and bake at 350° for 20 to 25 minutes.

FETTUCINE

1 12-oz. pkg. thin egg noodles, cooked, rinsed and drained
½ stick butter, cut into small pieces
2 egg yolks
½ c. or more of Parmesan cheese
1 t. salt
½ t. onion salt

Add butter, egg yolks and Parmesan cheese to hot noodles. Mix and toss with spoon and fork until well blended. Serve at once.

SALMON PATTIES

2 4½-oz. cans salmon
½ c. bread crumbs
Juice of 1 lemon
Salt
Pepper
1 T. chopped parsley
½ c. chopped onion
2 eggs

Mix all ingredients together. Shape into patties. Dip into additional beaten egg mixed with 1 tablespoon water and extra bread crumbs. Fry in butter.

CRAB DELIGHT

2 T. chopped green pepper
2 T. butter
2 T. flour
½ t. dry mustard
¼ t. salt
½ t. Worcestershire sauce
1 c. stewed tomatoes
1 c. grated cheese
¾ c. milk
1 c. shredded crab meat

Force tomatoes through a sieve. Sauté green pepper in butter for two minutes. Add flour, mustard, salt, Worcestershire sauce and stir until blended. Gradually stir in milk. Add tomatoes and cheese. Stir until cheese melts. Stir in crab meat. Serve in patty shells.

SHRIMPLY DELIGHTFUL

1½ lb. raw deveined shrimp
2 T. lemon juice
½ c. butter
½ c. bread crumbs
½ t. minced garlic or onion
2 T. chopped parsley
1 T. Parmesan cheese
1 T. oregano

Arrange shrimp on 9" buttered pie plate; sprinkle with lemon juice. Combine melted butter with bread crumbs, garlic or onion, parsley. Spoon over shrimp. Bake uncovered, at 350° for 15 minutes. Broil 3 minutes to brown the crumbs. Garnish with parsley and lemon.

ITALIAN RICE

½ c. quick-cooking rice
½ c. vegetable oil
½ c. celery
3 T. chopped parsley
2 c. chicken stock
½ t. salt
¼ c. chopped onion

Sauté celery and onion and parsley in oil. Add rice and chicken stock. Place in a casserole and bake in a 350° oven for 17 minutes.

OVEN BAKED RICE

1 c. rice
1 t. salt
½ c. margarine
1 c. beef consommé
1 c. water

Mix all ingredients together. Place in a buttered casserole and bake in a 350° oven for 45 minutes.

Note: For yellow rice, add 1 teaspoon turmeric to cooked rice.

CURRIED RICE

1 c. rice
3 c. chicken stock
1 onion, finely chopped
2 T. butter
2 t. salt
2 t. curry powder

Combine rice and chicken broth in a large saucepan. Bring to a boil, then simmer. Sauté onion in butter. Before the rice is tender and done, add the onion, salt and curry powder. Mix well; add more stock if needed. Place in a buttered dish and bake in a 300° oven for about 30 minutes. Serve with creamed chicken or veal.

Pictured opposite:
Shrimply Delightful

SPINACH CHEESE SOUFFLÉ

3 eggs
6 T. flour
1 10-oz. pkg. frozen chopped spinach, cooked and drained
1 lb. cottage cheese
½ lb. grated cheddar cheese
½ t. salt

Beat eggs; add flour and beat until smooth. Stir in remaining ingredients. Place in a well-buttered, 2 quart casserole. Bake, uncovered, at 350° for 1 hour. Serves 6.

Vegetables

CARROT RICE RING

1½ c. grated carrot
1 c. cooked rice
1 T. chopped onion
1 egg
1 c. grated American or cheddar cheese
Salt
Pepper

Place carrots in a saucepan; cover with hot water. Boil 5 minutes. Add remaining ingredients and pour into a buttered 4-cup ring mold. Bake at 350° for 45 minutes. Serve with creamed chicken or other vegetables in the center.

STUFFED TOMATOES

1 c. rice, partly cooked
1 small onion, finely chopped
½ c. raisins
Olive oil
Salt
Tomatoes

Sauté onion in olive oil; add salt, rice, and raisins. Scoop out the insides of tomatoes, but save the tops. Place filling in tomatoes, cover with tops. Bake in a little water at 350° for about 20 minutes or until tender. Broil for 2 minutes to brown slightly. Peppers can be substituted for tomatoes.

ZUCCHINI CASSEROLE

    2 lbs. zucchini squash, cut up
1¼ lbs. ground beef
    1 onion, chopped
    1 t. salt
    1 t. pepper
    ½ lb. American cheese, cubed
    1 10½-oz. can cream of mushroom soup

Simmer squash in a small amount of water until tender. Drain well. Brown beef and onion; add seasonings. Combine cubed cheese, squash and meat mixture. Place in buttered casserole and cover with undiluted cream of mushroom soup. Top with bread crumbs or broken potato chips. Bake at 350° for 45 minutes.

MUSHROOM RING

    1 lb. fresh mushrooms
    1 onion, finely chopped
    4 T. butter
    2 T. flour
    1 c. milk
    4 eggs, separated
       Salt and pepper

Wash and dry mushrooms; chop. Sauté mushroom and onion in 2 tablespoons butter for 5 minutes. Melt additional 2 tablespoons butter; stir in flour. Add milk; cook, stirring, until slightly thickened. Add beaten egg yolks. Remove from heat and fold in stiffly beaten egg whites. Pour into well-buttered and floured 4-6 cup ring mold. Place mold in a pan with 1 inch of water. Steam in a 350° oven for 30 to 40 minutes. Unmold and fill with creamed chicken or buttered vegetables.

DEVILED TOMATOES

    4 tomatoes, cut in halves
    2 hard-boiled eggs, riced
    1 T. vinegar
    ½ t. dry mustard
    1 T. mayonnaise

Combine eggs, vinegar, mustard and mayonnaise. Place equal portions of the egg mixture on top of each tomato half. Broil 5 minutes. Garnish with parsley.

CABBAGE AU GRATIN

    ½ head cabbage, coarsely chopped
    4 T. butter
    4 T. flour
1½ c. milk
    ½ t. salt
    ¾ c. shredded cheddar cheese
    ½ c. bread crumbs
    3 T. melted butter

Cook cabbage until tender; drain well. In a saucepan, melt butter. Add flour, milk and salt, stirring until thickened. Add cabbage and cheddar cheese. Pour into a buttered casserole and top with the crumbs which have been mixed with the melted butter. Bake at 350° for 20 minutes or until slightly browned on top.

BROCCOLI CHEESE BAKE

    1 10-oz. pkg. frozen chopped broccoli
    ¼ c. melted butter
    1 lb. large-curd cottage cheese
    6 eggs, separated
    ½ lb. cheddar cheese, cubed
    6 T. flour

Stir flour into melted butter. Add beaten egg yolks, broccoli and cottage cheese. Beat egg whites firm but not stiff. Fold egg whites and cheddar cheese into broccoli mixture. Bake in a 2-quart casserole at 350° for 1 hour.

CORN RING

    1 1-lb. can whole kernel corn, drained
    4 eggs, separated
    1 t. salt
    1 c. light cream

Beat egg yolks until thick and creamy. Add to corn with cream and salt. Fold in beaten egg whites. Pour in a 6-cup ring mold and set in a pan of hot water. Bake in a 350° oven for ½ hour, or until set as a custard. Fill center with colorful vegetables or chicken with mushrooms.

PARSLEY RING

1 c. cooked rice
1 c. minced parsley
2 eggs
½ c. melted butter
1 t. salt
1 c. cheddar cheese, cut into small pieces
1½ c. milk
1 t. onion juice or flakes

Mix together all ingredients and place in a well-buttered 6-cup casserole. Set casserole in a pan of hot water and steam for 1 hour in a 350° oven. Remove from oven and allow to sit for about 10 minutes before unmolding on a plate. Fill center with creamed chicken, peas and mushrooms.

MUSHROOM WOODCHUCK

½ c. butter
4 T. flour
2 c. milk
½ lb. grated cheddar cheese
2 4½-oz. cans sliced mushrooms
1 small jar sliced pimiento
1 green pepper, diced
6 hard-boiled eggs, cut up
Salt and pepper

Melt butter; add flour and blend. Stir in milk. Cook until thickened and cool. Add grated cheese, mushrooms, green pepper, eggs, and pimiento and seasonings. Serve on toasted English muffins or on chow mein noodles. Serves 6 to 8 guests.

HARVARD BEETS

1 1-lb. can small beets, quartered
2 T. butter
1 T. flour
½ t. salt
¼ c. orange juice
¼ c. beet juice
¼ c. sugar

Melt butter; blend in flour and salt. Stir in orange juice, beet juice, and sugar. Cook slowly until thickened. Add beets; serve hot.

POTATO PUFF

1½ c. cooked, mashed potatoes
¼ c. minced onion
2 t. salt
2 c. large-curd cottage cheese, drained
1 c. sour cream
3 eggs, separated
¼ c. pimiento, finely chopped
2 T. butter

Stiffly beat egg whites. Combine all ingredients except egg whites and butter. Mix thoroughly; fold in egg whites. Pour mixture in a casserole and top with butter. Bake at 350° for one hour.

BROCCOLI SOUFFLÉ

1 bunch of fresh broccoli or 1 pkg. frozen
1 c. mayonnaise
1 c. condensed cream of celery soup
6 eggs, beaten
1 small onion, grated
Salt and pepper to taste

If fresh broccoli is used, cut up into small pieces. Defrost frozen broccoli if used. Combine all ingredients. Pour into a 6-cup casserole. Place casserole in a pan of hot water and bake in a 300° oven for 45 minutes.

GREEN BEAN CASSEROLE

1 10-oz. pkg. frozen French-cut green beans
1 10½-oz. can cream of mushroom soup
1 can French-fried onion rings

Cook beans according to package directions. Drain well. Mix beans and soup; place in a casserole. Top with French fried onion rings. Bake in a 350° oven for 20 minutes.

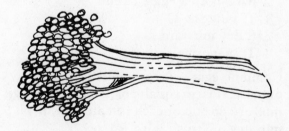

Pictured opposite:
Spaghetti Amore, p. 21

Salads and Dressings

SALMON SALAD

- 1 1-lb. can salmon, drained
- 2 T. vinegar
- 1 t. salt
  - Paprika
- 2 hard-boiled eggs
- 10 stuffed olives, sliced
- 1 t. sweet pickle relish
- ½ c. mayonnaise
- 2 T. chili sauce
- 2 T. unflavored gelatin
- ¼ c. milk
- ¼ c. hot milk
- 1 c. chopped celery
- ½ green pepper, diced

Soak gelatin in milk; dissolve in hot milk. Add remaining ingredients and place in a well-oiled mold. Crab meat or shrimp may be used in place of the salmon. Serve with salad dressing.

WILTED SPINACH OR LETTUCE

- 1 head lettuce or spinach
- 3 slices bacon, diced
- ¼ c. vinegar
- 1 t. sugar
- ½ t. salt

Wash, drain, and break spinach or lettuce into small pieces. Fry bacon slowly until crisp; remove and set aside. To bacon fat, add vinegar, sugar and salt. When dressing is sizzling hot, pour over the wilted vegetables. Top with the crisp bacon bits.

FROSTED MELON SALAD

Peel a whole medium-size cantaloupe; cut off one end and scoop out seeds. Fill with tomato aspic or fruit gelatin. Chill. Soften one 8-ounce package of cream cheese with a little milk and frost the outer side of the melon. Refrigerate and slice. Serve on lettuce or greens.

BING CHERRY MOLD

1 c. bing cherries, pitted and drained
1 3-oz. pkg. lemon jello
1 3-oz. pkg. cream cheese, softened
1½ c. boiling water
2 c. whipped cream
1 3-oz. pkg. cherry gelatin
2 c. cherry juice

Dissolve gelatin in boiling water; let thicken slightly. Add cream cheese and whipped cream. Dissolve cherry gelatin in boiling cherry juice. Cool; add cherries. Place lemon mixture in bottom of well-oiled ring mold. Top with second mixture. Serve with additional whipped cream.

FROZEN STRAWBERRY SALAD

2 6-oz. pkgs. strawberry gelatin
1½ c. boiling water
1 c. sour cream
2 10-oz. pkgs. frozen strawberries

Dissolve gelatin in boiling water; add strawberries. Spoon half of the mixture into oiled 4 or 6-cup ring mold. Pour sour cream over and top with remainder of strawberry gelatin.

APPLESAUCE MOLD

2 3-oz. pkgs. lime gelatin
½ c. boiling water
1 c. evaporated milk
2 c. applesauce
1 t. almond extract

Dissolve gelatin in water. Add remaining ingredients and pour into oiled ring mold. Serve with assorted fruits and a fruit dressing.

MELON FRUIT SALAD

Cut a cantaloupe in half, using the knife zigzag around the melon. Pull melon apart and remove seeds from center. Fill cavity with an assortment of fresh fruits blended with honey. Top with whipped cream. Serve with sandwiches.

JEWEL MOLD

1 6-oz. pkg. lemon gelatin
2 c. boiling water
2 c. cold water
2 No. 2½ cans fruit cocktail, drained

Dissolve gelatin in boiling water; add cold water (or juice from fruit cocktail) and stir. Refrigerate until slightly thickened. Add drained fruit and pour in a 6-cup, lightly greased mold. Refrigerate until set. To unmold, place in a sink of hot water for a few seconds.

TOMATO ASPIC

2 envelopes unflavored gelatin
1 c. cold water
1 c. ice water
2 8-oz. cans tomato sauce

Place cold water on gelatin, heat 2 to 3 minutes until thoroughly dissolved. Add ice water and tomato sauce. Pour in a 4-cup mold. Serve with shrimp, in a salad, or with cottage cheese.

EASY TOMATO ASPIC

1 c. water
1 3-oz. pkg. lime gelatin
1 16-oz. can tomatoes
1 T. vinegar
1 T. sugar

Dissolve gelatin in boiling water. Cut canned tomatoes into smaller pieces and heat. Stir gelatin, vinegar, and sugar into tomatoes. Pour into a 6" x 9" oiled pan. Serve in squares with salad dressing.

CHEESE DRESSING FOR FRUIT SALAD

1 3-oz. pkg. cream cheese, softened
½ c. currant jelly
   Juice of 1 lemon
¼ t. salt
½ c. whipped cream
½ c. chopped pecans

Combine cream cheese, jelly, juice, and salt, mixing well. Fold in whipped cream and nuts.

FRENCH DRESSING

1   clove garlic, finely chopped
1   T. salt
1½   t. dry mustard
½   t. paprika
1   10½-oz. can tomato soup
1   c. vegetable oil
1   c. vinegar
1   c. sugar

Blend in blender or shake in jar until smooth. Makes 2 pints.

RUM DRESSING FOR FRUITS

One package dessert topping mix made according to directions and whipped stiff. Add 16 marshmallows cut into quarters. Add a drop red coloring to tint a delicate pink and ½ teaspoon white rum or rum extract. Heap in a compote in center of a platter of fruit or molded gelatin.

THICK FRENCH DRESSING

¾   c. sugar
1   t. dry mustard
1½   t. paprika
1½   t. salt
⅓   c. vinegar
1   c. vegetable oil
1   t. onion salt

Mix together dry ingredients. Add oil and vinegar very slowly. Blend in blender for three minutes, until smooth and creamy.

CELERY SEED DRESSING

1   c. vegetable oil
9   T. sugar
¼   c. vinegar
2   T. celery seed
1   small onion, finely chopped

Place all ingredients in a jar. Cover and shake well. Refrigerate. Serve on a vegetable or fruit salad.

CREME DE CACAO DRESSING

4 T. white creme de cacao
½ t. sour cream
1 t. confectioners' sugar
2 t. grated lemon rind

Mix all ingredients together and serve on fresh fruit.

OIL MAYONNAISE

1 egg
1 t. dry mustard
1 t. salt
1 T. sugar
1½ c. vegetable oil
1 T. lemon juice
3 T. vinegar

Place first four ingredients in blender and beat a little. Slowly add oil, drop by drop at first until it blends, then add the remainder. Continue blending. Add lemon juice and vinegar. If mixture should separate, beat 1 egg with 1 tablespoon water and slowly add.

HORSERADISH SAUCE

1 pt. sour cream
½ t. salt
¾ c. applesauce
½ t. lemon juice
3 T. horseradish

Combine all ingredients and chill. Excellent served with ham.

EASY BARBECUE SAUCE

1 12-oz. can cola
1 c. tomato catsup
2 t. Worcestershire sauce

Mix ingredients well. Use as a barbecue sauce or to baste meats when roasting.

QUICK CHUTNEY

½ c. plum jam
¼ c. raisins
1 T. vinegar
½ t. pumpkin pie spice
2 T. brown sugar
¼ c. dates, finely chopped
¼ c. maraschino cherries

Heat all ingredients except cherries to boiling. Cool and stir in cherries. Serve with curry.

RUM RAISIN SAUCE

½ c. raisins
1 c. vinegar
2 small onions, finely chopped
1 bay leaf
6 peppercorns, crushed
2 T. currant jelly
2 oz. rum
2 c. any meat gravy

Parboil raisins in enough water to cover; drain. Combine vinegar, onions, bay leaf, and peppercorns. Boil until liquid is reduced by one half. Add jelly, rum, and meat gravy. Simmer for 10 minutes. Add raisins.

MUSHROOM WINE SAUCE

½ c. butter
1 lb. fresh mushrooms, sliced
1 T. onion flakes
Salt
Parsley flakes
½ c. flour
1 c. water
½ c. red wine

Melt butter; sauté mushrooms. Add onion flakes, flour, water and red wine. Cook until slightly thickened. Sprinkle with parsley flakes.

CRAB DELITES

4 English muffins
2 8-oz. pkgs. cream cheese
2 T. mayonnaise
2 6½-oz. cans crab meat
1 t. lemon juice
   Tomatoes
   Cheddar cheese, sliced

Cut English muffins in halves. Mix other ingredients together except tomatoes and cheese. Divide among the 8 muffin halves. Top with slice of tomato and slice of cheddar cheese. Bake at 225° for 1 hour.

Sandwiches

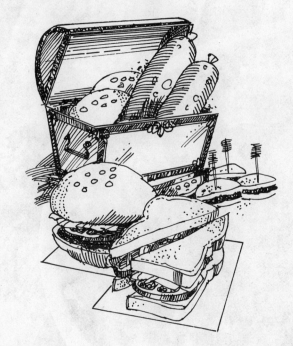

GLORIFIED DAGWOOD

Butter halves of hamburger buns; spread with prepared mustard. Put slice of boiled or baked ham on top, then a slice of cheddar cheese. Flaked crab meat, shrimp, or tuna on top with a thick slice of tomato. Spread all with mayonnaise. Broil 5 minutes and serve. Can be prepared a long time in advance and refrigerated until ready to pop into the oven.

STUFFED FRENCH BREAD

1 20" loaf French bread
½ c. mayonnaise
½ c. chopped parsley
1 4-oz. jar chopped pimiento
1½ c. chopped boiled or baked ham

Cut loaf of bread crosswise into four equal pieces. Hollow out each of the four sections. Combine remaining ingredients and pack mixture into the bread sections. Wrap in plastic wrap and chill several hours. To serve, cut into ½-inch slices.

CHICKEN ROLLS

1 t. candied ginger, chopped
1 t. salt
1 t. dry mustard
¼ t. curry powder
1 t. lemon juice
½ c. mayonnaise
¾ c. cooked, boned chicken, finely chopped
5 hard-boiled eggs, chopped
6 brown-and-serve rolls
2 T. dry coconut

Combine all ingredients except rolls and coconut. Toss together lightly. Cut rolls in half and remove the insides, leaving a ridge around like a shell. Fill each roll with the chicken mixture and sprinkle coconut on top. Place on cookie sheet and bake at 400° for 12 minutes, just long enough to brown the coconut. During the last five minutes, place the tops of rolls on with the crust side up. When serving, garnish with olives and parsley.

BROILED SANDWICH

For each sandwich:
1 slice bread
2 slices apple
1 slice cheddar cheese
2 small pieces bacon

Place bread on cookie sheet and toast under broiler. Turn over and place cheese on bread, top with apple slices and small strips of bacon. Broil about 4 inches from heat until bacon is done.

SHRIMP BOAT SANDWICHES

Scoop out the centers of hot dog buns. Fill with shrimp salad and top with grated cheddar cheese. Heat at 350° for 10 to 12 minutes.

BROILED MUSHROOM SANDWICHES

1 3-oz. pkg. cream cheese
1 T. butter
1 egg yolk
1 t. Worcestershire sauce
½ c. finely chopped fresh mushrooms
6 slices bread

Combine all ingredients, blending until smooth. Toast bread on one side. Spread mushroom mixture on the untoasted side and broil about 5 minutes.

CUCUMBER ROLLS

Bread slices
1 8-oz. pkg. cream cheese
1 T. mayonnaise
1 cucumber
1 T. chopped chives

Remove crusts from bread slices and place pieces between damp towels to soften. Cream softened cheese with mayonnaise. Peel and shred cucumber, squeeze out the juice and add to cheese mixture with chives. Spread some mixture on softened bread, and roll up very gently. Place open end down on plate and refrigerate until serving time.

SANDWICH ROYAL

Use 3 slices of bread for each sandwich, removing the crusts. Prepare any type of filling you desire, such as ham salad or egg salad. Alternate layers of filling and bread, pressing down each piece of bread over the filling. Cut the three layers in halves cross-wise and spread each top and sides with cream cheese combined with a little mayonnaise. Garnish top of each with glazed cherry half and a bit of candied pineapple for a stem and leaves. Serve with chicken or fruit salads.

Pictured opposite:
Easy Tomato Aspic, p. 33

BAKED APPLE MERINGUES

6 apples, baked and cooled
3 egg whites
  Salt
½ c. sugar
½ t. almond extract

Beat egg whites with salt until stiff. Gradually add sugar, beating until smooth and glossy. Place apples on cookie sheet. Thickly cover each with the meringue. Sprinkle with a few slivered almonds and bake at 325° for 15 minutes, or until light brown. Can be served as a dessert or as part of the meal.

Desserts

APPLE CRISP

6 apples
1 c. flour
½ c. butter
½ c. brown sugar
2 T. sugar
½ t. cinnamon

Peel, core and slice apples. Place in a buttered 8" x 12" pan. Mix together flour, sugars, butter and cinnamon until crumbly. Sprinkle over apples. Bake at 350° for 30 minutes. Serve warm topped with whipped cream, ice cream or milk.

PINEAPPLE FREEZE

1 3-oz. pkg. lemon gelatin
1 c. crushed pineapple
1 pt. vanilla ice cream

Prepare gelatin according to package directions. When partly congealed, add pineapple and softened ice cream. Freeze. Serve with cookies.

BAKED PEACHES

12 peach halves
2 oz. toasted almonds
1 T. grated orange rind
6 T. confectioners' sugar
¼ c. chopped dates
¼ c. chopped cherries
¼ c. sherry wine

Combine orange rind, sugar, dates, and cherries. Mound in peaches; top with nuts. Pour over sherry wine. Bake at 350° for 10 minutes. Use as a dessert or a garnish for meats.

FROZEN LEMON DESSERT

3 eggs, separated
¾ c. sugar
Juice and grated rind of 1 lemon
½ c. sugar
1 c. whipped dessert topping
Vanilla wafer crumbs

Beat egg yolks with ¾ cup sugar, lemon juice and rind in double boiler. Cook, stirring, until slightly thickened. Cool. Stiffly beat the egg whites with ½ cup sugar. Add dessert topping. Line a buttered 8" x 10" pan with vanilla wafer crumbs, saving a few for the top. Pour in the lemon mixture and top with the extra crumbs. A few chopped nuts can be sprinkled on top also.

EASY DESSERT

1 4½-oz. pkg. instant lemon pudding mix
1¼ c. milk
¼ c. Contreau
1½ c. whipped cream
1 angel food or chiffon cake

Beat instant pudding with milk and liqueurs until thickened. Fold in the whipped cream. Cut cake into 2 or 3 layers. Put filling between layers and on the top. Top can also be frosted with butter creme and marschino cherries.

RASPBERRY DESSERT

Vanilla wafers, crushed
1 lb. marshmallows
1 c. milk
1 t. gelatin
2 10-oz. pkgs. frozen raspberries
1 pt. whipped cream

Heat marshmallows with milk in double boiler until melted. Remove from heat. Dissolve gelatin in 1 tablespoon cold water; add to marshmallow mixture, stirring well. Fold in frozen berries and whipped cream. Pour onto crushed vanilla wafers in an 8" x 8" pan. Refrigerate. Serve in squares.

BAKED CUSTARD WITHOUT SUGAR

⅔ c. sweetened condensed milk
2¼ c. hot water
3 eggs, slightly beaten
¼ t. salt
¼ t. nutmeg

Mix milk with hot water and pour over eggs, adding salt and nutmeg. Pour into well-buttered custard cups and top with a bit more nutmeg. Place custard cups in a pan of hot water and bake in a 325° oven for 1 hour.

RHUBARB DESSERT

4 c. rhubarb, thinly sliced
2 c. sugar
½ c. maraschino cherries, cut up
2 eggs
3 T. cornstarch
1 c. sour cream
½ c. butter
1 c. sugar
1 c. flour

Combine rhubarb, 2 cups sugar and cherries, mixing well. Pour into a well-buttered 9" x 13" pan. Beat eggs; add cornstarch and sour cream, beating thoroughly. Pour over the fruit. Cut butter into flour and sugar until mixture resembles crumbs. Sprinkle on top. Bake in a 350° oven for 50 minutes.

APPLE DESSERT CRUNCH

4 c. diced apples
1 t. cinnamon
1 c. sugar
1 c. quick-cooking oats
1 c. brown sugar
⅔ c. flour
⅓ c. butter

Mix together the oats, brown sugar, flour, and butter. Combine apples, cinnamon, and sugar. Arrange in a well-buttered 8" x 11" pan. Sprinkle over the apple mixture. Bake at 350° for about 30 minutes. Serve warm, topped with whipped cream or ice cream.

BABA AU RUM

½ oz. yeast
3 T. sugar
½ t. salt
½ c. lukewarm water or milk
4 eggs, slightly beaten
2 c. flour or a little more for a soft dough
⅔ c. butter, softened

Mix yeast, sugar, salt, and water together until yeast is dissolved. Add remaining ingredients and beat well for 8 minutes. Cover and allow to rise for about 40 minutes or until doubled in bulk. Stir down and beat in butter. Butter a 9" ring mold or 2 dozen smaller ones. Fill half full, and let rise. Bake in a 400° oven for 10 minutes. Reduce heat to 350° and continue baking until cakes are golden brown in color. Dip into Rum Syrup and top with whipped cream.

RUM SYRUP

1 c. sugar
1 c. water
¼ c. rum

Combine all ingredients and bring to a boil.

QUICK ORANGE BABAS

1 pkg. yellow cake mix
¼ c. currants
¾ c. sugar
¾ c. water
¾ c. orange juice
3 T. grated orange peel

Mix cake mix according to package directions. Pour into a 4- or 6-cup well-buttered ring mold. Bake in a 375° oven for 25 minutes. Cool and carefully remove. Combine sugar, water, orange juice, and orange peel. Cook until sugar is dissolved. With a fork, prick cake on top and sides. While syrup is hot, slowly pour it over the cake. Chill and serve with Butter Creme Frosting or whipped cream.

EASY CHERRY TORTE

32 marshmallows
½ c. milk
2 c. whipped cream
Graham cracker crust
1 lb., 5 oz.-can cherry pie filling

Combine marshmallows and milk in top of double boiler. Melt over low heat; cool. Fold in whipped cream and pour onto graham cracker crust. Top with cherry pie filling. Refrigerate or freeze. Serve as is or top with a dab of whipped cream.

EASY DOBOS TORTE

3 pkgs. lady fingers, cut into halves
Butter Creme Frosting

Cover the bottom of an 8-inch pan with lady fingers. Spread with butter creme; top with another layer of finger halves. Alternate layers until all the lady fingers have been used. Frost sides and top with the remaining butter creme. Decorate with maraschino cherries. Refrigerate.

Pictured opposite:
Coconut Salad Strips, p. 55
Seasoned Croutons, p. 55
Nut Sticks for Fruit Salads, p. 55

CREAM CHEESE TART PASTRY

1 8-oz. pkg. cream cheese
¼ c. butter
1 c. flour
Salt

Combine all ingredients. Bake at 400° for 8 to 10 minutes. Can also be made into cheese straws. Makes 18 to 24 straws.

CHEESE TARTS

1 pkg. crumbled vanilla wafers
2 oz. cream cheese
½ c. sugar
3 eggs
1 t. vanilla

Place small paper cups in 15 to 18 muffin cups. Divide the vanilla wafer crumbs and put in the bottom of each cup. Cream softened cream cheese and sugar; add eggs and vanilla. Pour filling in each paper cup. Bake at 350° for 15 to 20 minutes. Top with a small amount of cherry pie filling and whipped cream. Fills 15 to 18 cups.

MACAROON TARTS

½ c. butter
¼ c. confectioners' sugar
1 c. flour
1 egg yolk
Raspberry jam

Cut butter into sugar and flour until crumbly. Stir in egg yolk, gather into a ball. Pat into buttered 1½-inch diameter tart tins. Drop ½ teaspoon raspberry jam into the bottom of each pastry-lined tart tin. Cream almond paste and sugar. Add vanilla, butter, and egg white. Stir in bread crumbs, beating well. (Mixture will be quite thick.) Spoon mixture into tart shells over raspberry jam. Fill to the top. Bake in a 350° oven for 20 to 25 minutes or until browned.

BUTTER CREME FROSTING

1 c. butter
1 c. sugar
1 t. vanilla
¾ c. flour
⅔ c. milk
½ c. cocoa

Cream together butter and sugar. Add vanilla, flour, milk and cocoa. Beat well.

CHOCOLATE DESSERT FONDUE

3 3-oz. bars milk chocolate
⅓ c. heavy cream
2 T. brandy or kirsch

In a double boiler, melt chocolate. Stir in cream and brandy. Pour into a fondue pot. Serve with assorted dippers, such as assorted fruits and cubes of angel food or sponge cakes.

SEMISWEET FONDUE

2 3-oz. bars milk chocolate
1 3-oz. bar bittersweet chocolate
⅓ c. heavy cream
¼ t. cinnamon
1 T. instant coffee

In a double boiler, melt chocolate. Add cream, cinnamon, and coffee. Pour into a fondue pot. Serve with banana slices, fruit sections, or cubes of sponge cake.

CHOCOLATE SAUCE

2 1-oz. squares semisweet chocolate
2 T. butter
1 5-oz. can evaporated milk
1 c. sugar
¼ t. salt
1 t. vanilla

Melt chocolate with butter in double boiler. Add milk, sugar and salt. Bring to a boil, stirring constantly. Remove from heat when slightly thickened. Add vanilla, cool and refrigerate. Serve hot or cold.

KAHLUA DESSERT

Roll scoops of vanilla ice cream in toasted coconut. Pour Kahlua over the top. Brandy or Creme de Cacao may also be used.

GRAHAM CRACKER CRUST

½ c. butter
½ c. sugar
2 c. graham cracker crumbs
1½ t. cinnamon

Melt butter; stir into remaining ingredients. Pat into a buttered tin. Can be frozen.

FOOLPROOF PIE CRUST

4 c. flour
1 T. sugar
2 t. salt
1¾ c. shortening
1 T. vinegar
1 egg
½ c. water

Mix together flour, sugar, salt and shortening with a fork. Stir in vinegar, egg and water. Mold into a ball with the hands. Chill 15 minutes. This amount is enough for two double crust pies and one pie shell. Keeps in the refrigerator for three days. Can also be frozen. This pastry never gets tough.

CHOCOLATE MINT PIE

3 1-oz. squares semisweet chocolate
½ c. butter
1 c. confectioners' sugar
2 eggs, slightly beaten
1 t. vanilla
½ t. peppermint extract
1 9" graham cracker crust

Melt chocolate; cool slightly. Cream butter with sugar; add eggs, vanilla, and extract. Add melted chocolate, beating well. Refrigerate until chilled. Beat on high for 2 minutes until very light and fluffy. Spread on a graham cracker crust. Refrigerate and top with whipped cream.

MILE-HIGH PIE

2 egg whites
1 c. sugar
¼ t. salt
1 10-oz. pkg. frozen strawberries
½ pt. whipped cream
1 9" graham cracker crust

In large bowl, beat egg whites for 15 minutes. Gradually add sugar and salt; beat another 15 minutes. Fold in frozen berries and whipped cream. Pour onto crust. Refrigerate overnight. Swirls of whipped cream can be added if desired.

IMPOSSIBLE PIE

4 eggs
2 c. milk
⅔ c. sugar
½ c. flour
½ c. margarine
1 t. vanilla
½ t. salt
1 c. coconut

Mix together all ingredients and blend for 15 seconds. Pour into well-buttered 9-inch plate. Bake in a 350° oven for 40 minutes.

LOW-CALORIE LEMON PIE

3 T. cornstarch
¾ t. granulated non-calorie sweetener
1 T. butter
½ c. water
3 eggs, separated
¼ c. sugar
1 t. grated lemon rind
¼ c. lemon juice
½ t. cream of tartar
¼ t. salt
2 T. plus 1 t. sugar
1 9" graham cracker crust

Combine cornstarch, sweetener, butter, water, egg yolks, sugar, lemon rind and juice. Cook over low heat, stirring constantly, until thickened. Set aside. Beat egg whites with cream of tartar until soft peaks form. Slowly beat in remaining sugar. Pour cooled lemon mixture on crust; top with meringue. Bake at 350° for 15 minutes.

FUDGE SUNDAE PIE

1 c. chocolate chips
¼ t. salt
1 c. evaporated milk
1 c. miniature marshmallows
   Vanilla wafer crumbs
1 qt. vanilla ice cream

Combine chocolate chips and evaporated milk. Melt over low heat. Remove from heat and add miniature marshmallows; stir until melted. Butter a 9-inch pie plate. Press vanilla wafer crumbs in pie plate. Spoon half of the ice cream on top. Pour over half of the chocolate mixture which has been cooled. Add another layer of ice cream then chocolate. Freeze 5 hours.

MACAROON PIE

3 eggs, separated
½ c. sugar
¼ t. salt
1 t. almond extract
½ c. chopped nuts
1 c. macaroon crumbs

Beat egg yolks; add sugar, salt, almond extract and nuts. Stir in crumbs. Stiffly beat egg whites and fold into egg yolk mixture. Pour into an 8-inch buttered pie pan. Bake in a 350° oven for 30 minutes. When serving, top with fresh strawberry halves and whipped cream.

LEMON SPONGE PIE

2 T. butter
1 c. sugar
   Juice and grated rind of 1 lemon
2 eggs, separated
3 rounded T. flour
¼ t. baking powder
   Pinch salt
1 c. milk

Cream butter with sugar; add beaten egg yolks, dry ingredients, lemon juice, rind, and milk. Fold in beaten egg whites. Pour into a buttered 9-inch pie plate and bake in a 350° oven for 45 minutes.

EASY STRAWBERRY PIE

1 c. water
1 c. sugar
2½ T. cornstarch
3 T. strawberry gelatin
1 qt. fresh strawberries, washed and hulled
1 9" baked pie crust

Combine water, sugar, and cornstarch in a saucepan. Cook, stirring constantly, until thick. Add the dry gelatin. Cool slightly. Arrange berries in pie crust. Pour gelatin over the berries. Serve chilled and topped with whipped cream.

Pictured opposite:
French Dressing, Cheese Dressing for fruit salad, p. 35

CHEESE PIE

2 c. salted pretzel crumbs
½ c. sugar
1 c. butter or margarine
1 8-oz. pkg. cream cheese
½ c. confectioners' sugar
2 c. whipped dessert topping

Reserve ½ cup of the pretzel crumbs. Combine crumbs, sugar and melted butter. Pat into a 9-inch pie plate. Cream together softened cream cheese and sugar. Stir in the dessert topping. Top with the reserved crumbs. Refrigerate.

MAGIC CHOCOLATE PIE

2 1-oz. squares unsweetened chocolate
1 11-oz. can sweetened condensed milk
½ t. vanilla
½ c. water
¼ t. salt

Melt chocolate in double boiler; add milk. Cook over boiling water, stirring constantly, for 5 minutes or until thick. Add water. Cool. Stir in vanilla. Pour in a baked 9-inch pie shell. Chill; serve topped with whipped cream.

QUICK GRASSHOPPER PIE

4 T. melted butter
24 chocolate wafers, crushed into crumbs
24 large marshmallows
½ c. milk
4 T. creme de menthe
2 T. white creme de cacao
1 c. whipped cream

Mix butter with chocolate wafers and pat into a buttered pie plate, pressing around sides and bottom. In a saucepan, combine marshmallows and milk. Melt over low heat; cool. Fold in the liqueurs and whipped cream. Pour on chocolate wafers crust. Freeze.

GLAZED RUM BANANAS

Melt a little butter and sauté quartered bananas. Sprinkle with brown sugar. Cover and cook until sugar is melted. Place in chafing dish. Sprinkle with warm rum, ignite and serve while blazing, either as is or over ice cream.

RUM SAUCE

4 egg yolks
½ c. confectioners' sugar
1½ t. rum
1 pt. whipped cream

Beat egg yolks with sugar; add rum and fold in whipped cream. Serve on angel food cake.

CHOCOLATE SAUCE

1 T. cocoa
1 c. sugar
4 T. flour
Pinch salt
1 t. butter
1 c. hot water
Vanilla

In a saucepan, combine all ingredients except vanilla. Cook, stirring constantly, until thickened. Remove from heat and stir in vanilla. Serve hot or cold.

ORANGE SAUCE

½ c. sugar
1 T. cornstarch
1 t. grated orange rind
1 c. water
2 T. orange juice
1 t. lemon juice

In a saucepan, combine sugar, cornstarch, water, and orange rind. Boil 5 minutes, stirring occasionally. Remove from heat and add orange juice and lemon juice. Serve chilled over berries.

CHOCOLATE CRUNCH

½ lb. semisweet chocolate
2 3-oz. cans chow mein noodles
1 t. vanilla

Heat chocolate in a double boiler until melted. Remove from heat. Add noodles and vanilla, stirring well to coat. Drop on waxed paper by teaspoons.

BUTTERSCOTCH LOG

1 6-oz. pkg. butterscotch chips
⅓ c. sweetened condensed milk
½ t. vanilla
⅓ c. chopped pecans

Melt butterscotch chips over low heat. Remove from heat and add the remaining ingredients. Chill. Form into a 12-inch roll on waxed paper. Mark the surface of the roll with a fork. Brush with 1 egg white mixed with 1 teaspoon water. Press pecan halves over the top. Chill and cut into ½-inch slices. Makes about 24 slices.

Candy

COCONUT BONBONS

½ c. light corn syrup
1 c. large marshmallows
4 to 5 c. shredded coconut
1 t. vanilla

Melt marshmallows in corn syrup in top of double boiler. Stir in vanilla and coconut. Form into ½-inch balls. Dip into fondant.

FONDANT

2 T. milk
1½ t. butter
2 c. confectioners' sugar (about)

Heat milk with butter. Stir in enough confectioners' sugar to make a thin icing. Tint any color desired. Dip each ball into fondant, then set on a rack to harden.

EASY FONDANT

2 T. butter or margarine
1 T. evaporated milk
1 egg white
4 c. confectioners' sugar
  Peppermint or vanilla extract

Mix together all ingredients, adding enough sugar to knead the mixture. Roll out on a confectioners' sugared board to about ¼ inch thick. Cut rounds, ½ inch in diameter. Fondant can be tinted with delicate coloring.

UNCOOKED FUDGE

3 1-oz. squares unsweetened chocolate
½ c. butter
4 c. confectioners' sugar
1 egg white
1 t. vanilla
16 large marshmallows, cut up
½ c. chopped nuts

Cream together butter and sugar. Add melted chocolate, egg white, and vanilla, mixing well. Fold in cut-up marshmallows and nuts. Drop by teaspoons on waxed paper. Refrigerate.

DIPPED CHOCOLATE FRUIT

Melt 6 semisweet chocolate squares in the top of a double boiler. Cool slightly. Dip fruits into the chocolate. Place on waxed paper; refrigerate to harden. If chocolate hardens during dipping, melt again over hot water. Fruits to use: grapes, stuffed dates, or strips of orange rind.

CHOCOLATE ROLL

⅓ c. mashed potatoes
1¾ c. sifted confectioners' sugar
2⅔ c. shredded coconut
½ t. vanilla
3 1-oz. squares semisweet chocolate, melted

Place mashed potatoes in a bowl with sugar, coconut, and vanilla. Stir until well blended; mixture will be stiff. Shape into a roll, 2 inches in diameter. Spread the melted chocolate over the roll. Chill and slice thin. Makes about 3 dozen slices.

COCONUT CARAMEL BALLS

3 c. dry cake crumbs
½ c. butter, softened
¼ c. brown sugar
1 t. vanilla
2 c. coconut
1 egg white

Mix together crumbs, butter, brown sugar, and vanilla. Shape into balls about one inch in diameter. Beat egg white with 1 teaspoon water. Dip each ball into egg white then into coconut. Refrigerate to become a bit firmer.

FRUIT SLICES

1½ c. seedless raisins
1 c. dried apricots
1 c. figs
1½ c. pitted dates
12 candied cherries
1 c. candied orange rind
1½ c. walnuts
5 T. orange juice
⅓ c. walnuts

Chop fruits and 1½ cups walnuts in blender or food chopper. Add enough orange juice to hold ingredients together. Shape into a roll about 1½ inches in diameter. Roll in the remaining chopped nuts. Chill and cut into ½-inch slices.

*Pictured opposite:
Crab Delites, p. 37*

SUGARPLUMS

Steam apricots or prunes on a rack in a kettle over water for 15 minutes or until tender. Cool; slit lengthwise and stuff with nuts or softened marshmallows. Roll moist fruit in granulated sugar. Use as a garnish for a meat or fruit plate.

MINCEMEAT APPLES WITH A SNOWMAN

6 apples
½ c. sugar
3 c. water
Red food coloring
1 jar mincemeat

Peel and core apples. Combine sugar, water, and food coloring in a large saucepan. Stand apples in saucepan and simmer until apples are tender. Remove and invert to drain. Place in baking pan and fill apples with mincemeat. Serve warm around Hard Sauce Snowman.

Garnishes

HARD SAUCE SNOWMAN

½ c. butter, creamed
1 egg white
3 to 3½ c. confectioners' sugar
1 t. rum extract

Cream all together. Make a ball of ¾ of the mixture. Place on a plate. Form a ball of the smaller amount and put on top for the head. Use 2 cloves for the eyes, 1 for the nose and a piece of cherry for the mouth. Raisins for coat buttons. Put a toothpick through two dates, using one for each arm. Flatten a date and form it into a round piece. Put a toothpick through a cherry and through the date placing it on an angle as a tam o' shanter. Place snowman in center of tray of warm apples. Each guest spoons some of the hard sauce on the apple. Delicious.

GRAPEFRUIT ROSE

Pare yellow rind from grapefruit, keeping rind in a long thin strip. Roll the rind tightly. Holding at the center, turn a bit of the rind inward. Continue turning around and inward until a rose is formed. Secure with several toothpicks through the base. Holding the rose by the toothpick, dip it into red food coloring, then place on paper toweling to drain. Use as a garnish surrounded with several sprigs of curly endive. Will keep refrigerated for several days.

DATE STRAWBERRIES

5 T. margarine or butter
¼ c. sugar
1 lb. dates, cut up
1 t. vanilla
2½ c. rice crispies

Combine margarine, sugar and dates in a saucepan. Boil for 10 minutes. Cool and add vanilla. Add rice crispies. Mix well. Shape into 72 balls, flattening top and forming a point to resemble a strawberry. Dip each into red granulated sugar. Top with a plastic hull which can be purchased at a baker's supply store, or a bit of green parsley tucked in with a toothpick. The berries can also be dipped into Quick Fondant instead of red sugar.

QUICK FONDANT

2 T. milk
1½ t. butter
2 c. confectioners' sugar
Red food coloring

Combine all ingredients, stirring until smooth. Dip berries in the fondant, stand on end. Have green frosting for the stem.

FANCY LEMON SLICES

With the prongs of a fork, score the sides of a lemon. Slice thin and serve with iced tea. By cutting halfway through a lemon slice and giving it a twist, it looks very pretty on salads.

EASY FONDANT

2 T. butter or margarine
1 T. evaporated milk
2 egg whites
4 c. confectioners' sugar
1 t. peppermint or vanilla extract

Mix together all ingredients, adding enough sugar to knead mixture. Roll out to ¼ inch thick, on a board sprinkled with confectioners' sugar. Cut rounds 1½ inch in diameter. If desired, tint dough with food coloring and decorate with tiny flowers squeezed from a pastry tube. Makes about 100 pieces.

MARSHMALLOW GARDENIA

4 large marshmallows for each flower
Lemon leaves from a florist

Cut each marshmallow into five pieces. The outer edges will curl up. These are to be used for the center of the flower. On waxed paper, place 5 petals in a circular shape, pressing down the center. Place another row of 5 petals on top of the first group. Then three, finally two, using the curled up one. Cut one small piece in half lengthwise, roll it up tightly and place in the center, pressing down a bit. Lift up the whole flower and place on a lemon leaf, which resembles a gardenia leaf. Can be used on a salad or dessert plate, a cookie tray or, by adding a tiny bow, as a corsage. Nice for showers.

CANDIED ROSE PETALS

Rose petals
1 c. sugar
¾ c. water

Wipe rose petals dry and cut out the white base of the petal with scissors. Boil sugar and water until it spins a thread when spoon is lifted from the syrup; remove from heat. Pour syrup into a bowl sitting on a bed of crushed ice. When syrup begins to crystallize, dip each petal into syrup to coat. Shake off surplus and place on waxed paper to dry. As the petals begin to harden, dust with confectioners' sugar.

SUGARED ROSE PETALS

Prepare rose petals as in above recipe. Brush each with egg white slightly beaten with 1 teaspoon water. Place on waxed paper overnight to dry. The next day, repeat with the other side. When thoroughly dried, put in a glass jar for future use. Serve 2 or 3 pinched together on the top of the cake or a dessert.

DRIED FRUIT ON SKEWERS

Steam apricots, prunes and whole figs in a sieve over boiling water. Place on a skewer, alternating fruit. Brush with melted butter and place on a rack in a 400° oven for 3 to 5 minutes. Arrange filled skewers around meat.

EDIBLE NAPKIN RINGS

Use crescent roll dough, and separate rolls, placing on a breadboard, flattening with a rolling pin. Cut each in half. Cover an empty paper towel roll with foil and butter it well. Put the pieces of dough around the roll, making a slit on the widest edge to slip the pointed end through. Brush with egg yolk and water; place rolls on a buttered tin and bake at 375° for about 8 minutes. Immediately and carefully, remove napkin rings. Cool and insert napkins.

ONION MUM

Peel brown outer covering of onion. Cut enough from the stem end to make onion stand level. With a sharp knife, cut from the top to within a half inch of the bottom. Continue slicing onion lengthwise until it is divided into small sections. Dip onion into yellow food coloring. Surround with endive or greens.

COCONUT SALAD STRIPS

Remove crusts from day-old bread and cut into one-inch strips. Spread with sweetened condensed milk and roll in coconut. Bake at 375° for about 15 minutes or until light brown in color.

SEASONED CROUTONS

30 slices day-old bread, cubed
⅓ c. vegetable oil
3 T. instant minced onion
3 T. parsley
¾ t. sage
1 t. garlic salt
½ t. pepper

Spread out bread cubes on a large baking sheet. Combine remaining ingredients and sprinkle over cubes. Toast at 300° for 40 to 45 minutes. Cool and store in a covered jar.

NUT STICKS FOR FRUIT SALADS

Cut a loaf of unsliced bread into 1" slices; remove crusts. Spread both sides of each slice with creamed butter and roll in chopped nuts. Cut into one-inch lengths. Refrigerate or freeze. Place under broiler to brown being careful not to burn. Equal amounts of butter and brown sugar can be creamed and spread on strips of bread. Bread sticks can also be dipped into melted butter and topped with poppy seed or sesame seed and baked at 300° for ½ hour.

Pictured opposite:
Stuffed French Bread, p. 37

Sweet
Basil

Chives

Marjoram

Mint

Parsley

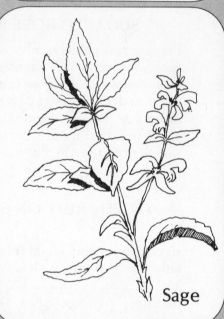

Sage

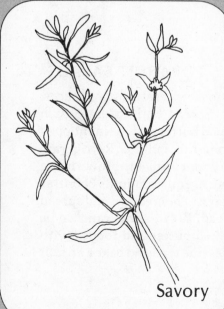

Savory

Tarragon

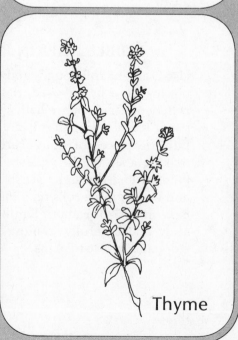

Thyme

HERBS	Use with:
Basil	Meat, fish, egg, cheese and tomato dishes.
Dill	Salads, soups and vegetable dishes.
Marjoram	Stews, soups, poultry, fish or lamb dishes.
Oregano	Salads, egg, meat and tomato dishes.
Rosemary	Stews, soups, fish, lamb, beef and potato dishes.
Sage	Poultry, meat, stews and cheese dishes.
Savory	Meat, poultry, dressings and sauces.
Tarragon	Sauces, salads, poultry, meat, eggs and tomato dishes.
Thyme	Soups, stews, meats, eggs and tomato dishes.
Mint	Candy, ice cream, icing, jelly.
Chives	Soups, sauces, salads, garnish, fish dishes.
Parsley	Soups, sauces, stuffings, meat and fish dishes.

TIMETABLE FOR ROASTING MEATS

Remove roasts from oven 20-30 minutes prior
to serving as they can be carved more easily.

CUT	WEIGHT (lbs.)	OVEN TEMP. (°F.)	MEAT THERMOMETER READING (°F)	MINUTES PER POUND
BEEF - Standing Rib	4-8	325	140 - rare	18 - 20
			160 - medium	22 - 25
			170 - well	27 - 30
Rolled Rib	4-6	325	140 - rare	28 - 30
			160 - medium	32 - 35
			170 - well	37 - 40
Rolled Rump	4-6	325	140 - rare	25 - 30
			160 - medium	32 - 35
Sirloin Tip	3-5	325	140 - rare	30
			160 - medium	35
Fillet	4-5	425	140 - rare	10
VEAL - Leg	5-8	325	170 - 180	35
Loin	4-6	325	170 - 180	35 - 40
Rolled Shoulder	4-6	325	170 - 180	40 - 45
PORK - Loin	2-7	325	185	35 - 45
Shoulder	5	325	185	40 - 45
Crown Roast	6-7	325	185	45 - 50
Uncooked - Whole Ham	8-20	325	160	18 - 20
Shank	4-8	325	160	35 - 0
Picnic	4-10	325	170	35 - 40
Precooked - Whole Ham	8-20	325	130	15
Shank	4-8	325	130	15 - 20
Picnic	4-10	325	130	25 - 35
Canadian Bacon		325	170	35 - 40
LAMB - Leg	5-8	325	165 - 170 rare	25 - 30
			175 - 180 medium	30 - 35
Rolled Shoulder	3-5	325	175 - 180	35 - 45
Crown Roast	4-6	325	175 - 180	35 - 45

Baked Apple Meringues, p. 40
Kahlua Dessert, p. 45

Hints

You'll do the best entertaining, and make your guests happiest, when you do what you really like to do. So, first of all, decide what kind of party it will be. Formal or informal? Indoors or out? Large or small? What to serve: full-meal, light refreshments, late-evening buffet?

Follow a written plan. You'll save time if you take time to write everything down—from the guest list, to the timetable for cooking.

Pick a theme. Set the mood. Make your party a little different from anyone else's, whether it's celebrating a birthday, anniversary, job promotion, or just for the fun of it.

Choose guests carefully. They should share some mutual interests. Mix up talkers and listeners. Let the spirit of friendship prevail.

Get out invitations a week or two ahead. Telephone or write a note. In both cases be specific about time, date, place, anything out of the ordinary about dress (sport clothes, costume, black tie), any special information about the occasion (if it's gift-giving, be explicit).

Plan what you'll serve. Your menu is all-important. No monochromatic menus, please! Get good color contrasts, but make sure foods in the same course do not clash. Contrast hot dishes with cold; soft foods with crisp; bland with strong-flavored. Vary the cooking method; for instance, no completely fried dinners. Enhance a colorless dish with a sauce or colorful garnish.

Plan variety here too. A creamy-sauced food needs something crisp and crunchy. You might add the crunch right in the sauce, with water chestnuts, slivered nuts or celery; in the vegetable course or with a relish tray. Keep a texture contrast throughout the meal, as well as within each course. Top off a heavy meal with a light dessert, and vice versa.

Include both tart and sweet, but save the very sweet for the end of the meal. One strong flavor or spiced dish is usually enough in one meal. Do not repeat flavors in the same meal (such as tomatoes, onions, or nutmeats).

Even if you can get by serving the same old standbys—don't. Hamburger can be served as Swedish meatballs, individual meat loaves, spaghetti or lasagna. Try new recipes using ingredients you know everyone likes. Combining foods is an easy way to create new dishes: mix two different cans of soup together; combine carrots with scallions, peas with dill, green beans with almonds.

Choose food that suits the occasion. Be realistic about what you can prepare well. Use recipes that you have already tested. Plan foods that don't require a lot of last minute fuss. Ideally, choose ones that can be fully or partially prepared early in the day.

Make a shopping list. Include everything you will need, from cocktail napkins to candles.

Plan the table setting early. This is fun to do when you have enough time—and aren't polishing silver when you should be putting the finishing touches on the flowers for the centerpiece. Work out a theme or color scheme, and make sure you have all the dishes, linens, and silver to carry it out. Try to set the table in the morning or the night before.

Clear a counter for soiled dishes. Out of sight of guests, please.

Set a schedule for yourself. Plan to be ready one half hour ahead. This will give you time to catch your breath before the guests arrive.

ACKNOWLEDGMENT

"Hints" from Festive Foods, copyright 1969, Wisconsin Gas Company, Milwaukee, Wisconsin.

EQUIVALENT AMOUNTS

Apples: 1 pound = 3 medium

Baking chocolate:
   1 square = 1 ounce or 5 tablespoons grated

Bread: 1 pound loaf = 18 slices

Butter or margarine: 1 pound = 2 cups
   1 stick or ¼ pound = ½ cup

Cheese (American, cheddar):
   1 pound = 4 cups grated

Cottage cheese: 1 pound = 2 cups

Eggs: 5 whole = 1 cup
   8 whites = about 1 cup
   16 yolks = about 1 cup

Flour, all purpose: 1 pound = 4 cups

Flour, cake: 1 pound = 4¾ cups

Lemon juice:
   1 medium lemon = 3 tablespoons juice

Lemon rind: 1 medium lemon =
                1 tablespoon grated rind

Noodles: 1 cup raw = 1¼ cups cooked

Macaroni: 1 pound = 3 cups uncooked
   1 cup = 2 cups cooked

Meat: 2 cups diced = 1 pound

Milk, evaporated:
   one 6-ounce can = ⅔ cup
   one 14½-ounce can = 1⅔ cups

Potatoes: 1 pound = 3 medium

Rice: 1 pound = 2⅓ cups uncooked
   1 cup raw = 3 cups cooked

Sugar: Brown — 1 pound =
   2¼ cups firmly packed
   Confectioners' — 1 pound = 3½ cups
   Granulated — 1 pound = 2 cups

Tomatoes: 1 pound = 3 medium

Vegetable shortening: 1 pound = 2 cups

COOKERY TERMS

Appetizer: Food served before the first course of a meal.

Brown: To make a food a brown color by frying, sautéing, broiling or baking.

Cream: To blend butter and sugar by stirring or beating.

Dice: To cut into small pieces.

Garnish: To add decorative color to food.

Grease: To rub a baking pan with fat, butter or oil.

Knead: To work dough until smooth and pliable.

Marinate: To soak food in a seasoned liquid for flavor.

Melt: To liquefy by heat.

Mince: To chop into fine pieces.

Sauté: To cook food quickly with fat, butter or margarine.

Scald: To bring liquid to a temperature just below the boiling point.

Whip: To beat rapidly.

MEASUREMENTS

1 tablespoon = 3 teaspoons
1 fluid ounce = 2 tablespoons
¼ cup = 4 tablespoons
⅓ cup = 5⅓ tablespoons
½ cup = 8 tablespoons
⅔ cup = 10⅔ tablespoons
¾ cup = 12 tablespoons
1 cup = 16 tablespoons or 8 fluid ounces
1 pint = 2 cups
1 quart = 2 pints or 4 cups
1 pound = 16 ounces
¾ pound = 12 ounces
½ pound = 8 ounces
¼ pound = 4 ounces

CONTENTS OF CANS

Size	Amount
#300	1¾ cups
1 tall	2 cups
303	2 cups
2	2½ cups
2½	3½ cups
3	4 cups
10	12-13 cups

Index

Butterscotch Log, p. 49
Uncooked Fudge, p. 51

Notes